D0949857

Garden
Magic

—

JOHN TRAIN
AND
LINDA KELLY

DISTRIBUTED BY
ANTIQUE COLLECTOR'S CLUB

—

EASTHAMPTON, MA　　　　　　　　　WOODBRIDGE, U.K.

Packaging and photo research: M.T. Train
Book design: Luisa Vanzo/
Jaques Vanzo Design Consultancy
Cover by: Natasha Tibbott, Our Designs, Inc.
Printing and binding: Print finishing Srl. Milano
©2013 M.T.T./Scala Books
ISBN: 9781905377688

Saint Fiacre, born in Ireland,
6th century, patron saint of
gardens and gardeners;
also coachmen.

INTRODUCTION

Creating beauty is a glorious experience, bringing happiness not only to the creator but also to all those who see the creation. And reading about it can also be great fun.

Flowers exist to be beautiful and attractive, first to the birds and bees; it is our good luck that we can share in the joy of their exuberant appeal. That is why we fill our houses with them and offer them to those we love.

Describing the joy of gardens has been a pleasure for prose writers, poets and painters since earliest times, as the selections in this book delightfully reveal.

—

J.T.

JOY

If you want to be happy for a day,
get drunk.

if you want to be happy for a week,
get married.

if you want to be happy for life,
become a gardener.

———

CHINESE PROVERB

ADVICE

If you have two pennies,
spend one on a loaf
and one on a flower.

The bread will give you life,
the flower a reason for living.

—

CHINESE PROVERB

GREEN FINGERS

Green fingers are the extension
of a verdant heart.

———

RUSSELL PAGE

WISHES

I never had any desire so strong and so like
covetousness, that I might be master of a small
house and a large garden.

———

ABRAHAM COWLEY

TREASURES

If you have a garden and a library you have
everything you want.

———

CICERO

HOW TO LIVE

Live as if you will die tomorrow.
Garden as if you will live for ever.

———

ANON

An 18th Century Garden Scene

NEWS

Gwendolen. Are there many interesting walks in the vicinity, Miss Cardew?

Cecily. Oh! yes! a great many. From the top of one of the hills quite close one can see five counties.

Gwendolen. Five counties! I don't think I should like that; I hate crowds.

Cecily. (Sweetly.) I suppose that is why you live in town? (**Gwendolen** bites her lip, and beats her foot nervously with her parasol.)

Gwendolen. (Looking round.) Quite a well-kept garden this is, Miss Cardew.

Cecily. So glad you like it, Miss Fairfax.

Gwendolen. I had no idea there were any flowers in the country.

Cecily. Oh, flowers are as common here, Miss Fairfax, as people are in London.

——

OSCAR WILDE
THE IMPORTANCE OF BEING EARNEST

THE SWALLOW AND
THE PRINCE

"What a strange thing!" said the overseer of the workmen at the foundry. "This broken lead heart will not melt in the furnace. We must throw it away." So they threw it on a dust-heap where the dead Swallow was also lying.

"Bring me the two most precious things in the city," said God to one of His Angels; and the Angel brought Him the leaden heart and the dead bird.

"You have rightly chosen," said God, "for in my garden of Paradise this little bird shall sing for evermore, and in my city of gold the Happy Prince shall praise me."

OSCAR WILDE
THE HAPPY PRINCE

GREEN THOUGHT

What wondrous life is this I lead!
Ripe apples drop about my head;
The luscious clusters of the vine
Upon my mouth do crush their wine;
The nectarine and curious peach
Into my hands themselves do reach;
Stumbling on melons as I pass,
Insnared with flowers, I fall on grass.

Meanwhile the mind, from pleasure less,
Withdraws into its happiness:
The mind, that ocean where each kind
Does straight its own resemblance find;
Yet it creates, transcending these,
Far other worlds, and other seas;
Annihilating all that's made
To a green thought in a green shade.

—

ANDREW MARVELL
THE GARDEN

Blackbird.

BALANCE

I value my garden more for being full of
blackbirds than of cherries, and very humbly
give them fruit for their song.

—

JOSEPH ADDISON

TRIBUTE

The Dahlia you brought to our isle
Your praises forever should speak
Mid gardens as bright as your smile
And in colour as bright as your cheek.

———

LORD HOLLAND TO LADY HOLLAND
(who is said to have introduced the dahlia to England)

THE CHERRY

Lovliest of trees, the cherry now
Is hung with blossom on the bough,
And stands about the woodland ride
Wearing white for Easter tide...

———

A.E. HOUSMAN

THE VAUXHALL
PLEASURE GARDENS

The gardens' great attraction arises from their being splendidly illuminated at night with about 15,000 glass lamps. These being tastefully hung among the trees, which line the walks, produce an impression similar to that which is called up on reading some of the stories in the Arabian Nights Entertainments. On some occasions there have been upwards of 19,000 persons in them, most of whom are well dressed, and this immense concourse, seen in connection with the illuminated walks, adds not a little to the brilliant and astonishing effect of the whole scene.

EDINBURGH ENCYCLOPEDIA, 1830

An 1809 print
from Vauxhall Gardens

SCENTS I

With a wildly excited Benedicò bounding ahead of him he went down the short flight of steps into the garden, which was exhaling scents that were cloying, fleshy and slightly putrid, like the aromatic liquids distilled from the relics of certain saints, the carnations superimposed their pungence on the formal fragrance of roses and the oily emanations of magnolias drooping in corners; and somewhat beneath it all was a faint smell of mint mingling with a nursery whiff of acacia and a jammy one of myrtle; from a grove beyond the wall came an erotic waft of early orange-blossom...

SCENTS II

It was a garden for the blind; a constant offence to the eyes, a pleasure strong if somewhat crude to the nose. The Paul Neyron roses, whose cuttings he had himself bought in Paris, had degenerated; first stimulated and then enfeebled by the strong if languid pull of Sicilian earth, burnt by apocalyptic Julys, they had changed into objects like flesh-coloured cabbages, obscene and distilling a dense almost indecent scent which no French horticulturist would have dared hope for.

The Prince put one under his nose and seemed to be sniffing the thigh of a dancer from the Opera. Benedicò, to whom it was also proffered, drew back in disgust and hurried off in search of healthier sensations amid dead lizards and manure.

GIUSEPPE TOMASI DI LAMPEDUSA
THE LEOPARD

PROSPECT

I tremble with pleasure when I think that on the very day of my leaving prison both the laburnum and the lilac will be blooming in the gardens and that I shall see the wind stir into restless beauty the swaying gold and purple of its plumes, so that all the air shall be Arabia for me.

—

OSCAR WILDE
DE PROFUNDIS

SING AGAIN

We'll gather lilacs in the spring again
And walk together down an English lane
Until our hearts have learned to sing again
When you come home once more...

—

IVOR NOVELLO
THE ENCHANTED HOUR

THE VILLA

The villa was small and square, standing in its tiny garden with an air of pink-faced determination. Its shutters had been faded by the sun to a delicate creamy-green, cracked and bubbled in places. The garden, surrounded by tall fuchsia hedges, had the flower-beds worked in complicated geometrical patterns, marked with smooth white stones. The white cobbled paths, scarcely as wide as a rake's head, wound laboriously round beds hardly larger than a big straw hat, beds in the shape of stars, half-moons, triangles, and circles, all overgrown with a shaggy tangle of flowers run wild. Roses dropped petals that seemed as big and smooth as saucers, flame-red, moon-white, glossy, and unwrinkled; marigolds like broods of shaggy suns stood watching their parent's progress through the sky. In the low growth the pansies pushed their velvety, innocent faces through the leaves, and the violets drooped sorrowfully under their heart-shaped leaves. The bougainvillea that sprawled luxuriously over the tiny front balcony was hung, as though for a carnival, with its lantern-shaped magenta flowers. In the darkness of the fuchsia-hedge a thousand ballerina-like blooms quivered expectantly. The warm air was thick with the scent of a hundred dying flowers, and full of the gentle, soothing whisper and murmur of insects. As soon as we saw it, we wanted to live there – it was as though the villa had been standing there waiting for our arrival. We felt we had come home...

In between keeping a watchful eye on us all, Mother was settling down in her own way. The house was redolent with the scent of herbs and the sharp tang of garlic and onions, and the kitchen was full of a bubbling selection of pots, among which she moved, spectacles askew, muttering to herself... When she could drag herself away from the kitchen, she would drift happily about the garden, reluctantly pruning and cutting, enthusiastically weeding and planting.

GERALD DURRELL
MY FAMILY AND OTHER ANIMALS

SUNFLOWER

Ah, Sun-flower! Weary of time
Who countest the steps of the sun;
Seeking after that sweet golden clime
Where the traveller's journey is done.

———

WILLIAM BLAKE

ACHIEVEMENT

By the time one is eighty, it is said, there is no
longer a tug of war in the garden with the May
flowers hauling like mad against the claims of the
other months. All is at last in balance and all is
serene. The gardener is usually dead, of course.

———

HENRY MITCHELL
THE ESSENTIAL EARTHMAN

AHMED'S FÊTE

Ahmed III's (1673-1736) fête of spring, the Tulip Fête, in the gardens of the Grand Seraglio came for a while to outshine in importance the established religious feasts of Islam. It was held always in the month of April on two successive evenings, preferably by the light of a full moon. The Sultan covered over like a conservatory a part of his gardens where the parterres of tulips were planted. Here ranged on shelves were countless vases of the flowers, carefully chosen and placed for their harmonizing colours and shapes, interspersed with minute lamps of coloured glass and glass globes filled with liquids of different colours, so as to shine as it were with their own light. On the branches of the trees, combining aviary with conservatory, were cages of canaries and rare singing birds. The Sultan sat throned in the center beneath an imperial pavilion, receiving homage. On the second evening the entertainment was for the ladies of the harem, whom he received alone, entertaining them with music and poetry and song and the dancing of his slaves, while turtles wandered through the gardens with candles on their backs, to light up the tulips. Sometimes there was a treasure hunt – as for Easter eggs in Europe – with coloured bonbons and trinkets concealed amid the flowers, and the concubines fluttering hither and thither, "tiptoeing through the tulips," as it were, in search of them. Ibrahim Pasha himself admired above all a variety named "Blue Pearl," offering handsome rewards to anyone who could acclimatize it, and covering it with white veils to protect it from the sun in hot weather.

LORD KINROSS
THE OTTOMAN CENTURIES

DISTRACTION

You can bury a lot of troubles digging in the dirt.

———

ANON.

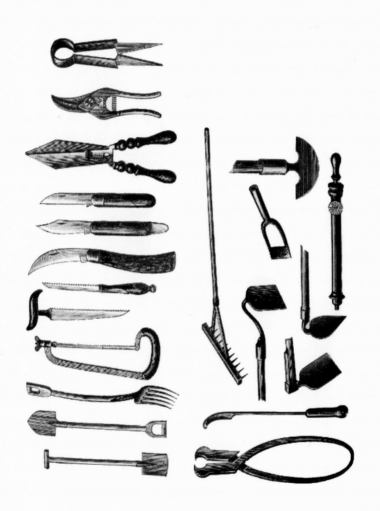

ACACIAS

That last week the syringa came out at San Salvatore, and all the acacias flowered.

No one had noticed how many acacias there were until one day the garden was full of a new scent, and there were the delicate trees, the lovely successors to the wisteria, hung all over their trembling leaves with blossom. To lie under an acacia tree that last week and look up through the branches at its frail leaves and white flowers quivering againt the blue of the sky, while the last movement of the air shook down their scent, was a great happiness. Indeed the whole garden dressed itself gradually toward white and grew more and more scented. There were the lilies, as vigorous as ever, and the white stocks and white pinks and white banksia roses, and the syringa and the jasmine, and at last the crowning fragrance of the acacias. When, on the first of May, everybody went away, even after they had got to the bottom of the hill and passed through the iron gates out into the village they could still smell the acacias.

ELIZABETH VON ARNIM
THE ENCHANTED APRIL

Thrush on branch.

SINGING

Did you not hear my Lady
Go down the garden singing,
Blackbird and thrush are silent
To hear the alleys ringing.
O see you not my Lady
Out in the garden there,
Shaming the rose and the lily
For she is twice as fair.
Though I am nothing to her
Though she must rarely look at me
And though I could never woo her
I love her till I die.
Surely you hear my Lady
Go down the garden singing,
Silencing all the songbirds
And setting the alleys ringing.
But surely you see my Lady
Out in the garden singing,
Rivaling the glittering sunshine
With a glory of golden hair.

—

ENGLISH WORDS TO HANDEL'S
"SILENT WORSHIP"

TULIP WARS

As I sat in the porch, I heard the voices of two or three persons, who seemed very earnest in discourse.

My curiosity was raised when I heard the names of Alexander the Great and Artaxerxes; and as their talk seemed to run on ancient heroes, I concluded there would not be any secret in it; for which reason I thought I might very fairly listen to what they said.

After several parallels between great men, which appeared to me altogether groundless and chimerical, I was surprised to hear one say that he valued the Black Prince more than the Duke of Vendôme. How the Duke of Vendôme should become a rival of the Black Prince, I could not conceive: and was more startled when I heard a second affirm, with great vehemence, that if the Emperor of Germany was not going off, he should like him better than either of them. He added, that though the season was so changeable, the Duke of Marlborough was in blooming beauty. I was wondering to myself from whence they had received this odd intelligence: especially when I heard them mention the names of several other generals, as the Prince of Hesse and the King of Sweden, who, they said, were both running away. To which they added, what I entirely agreed with them in, that the Crown of France was very weak, but that the Marshal Villars still kept his colours. At last, one of them told the company, if they would go along with him, he would show them a Chimney-Sweeper and a Painted Lady in the same bed, which he was sure would very much please them.

—

RICHARD STEELE
TATLER, 1709

MY GRANDMOTHER'S GARDEN

The garden could hardly be called a garden; it was large, wild and not too well kept. There were fruit trees amongst the flowers, here a pear tree, there a currant bush, so that one could either smell a rose, crush a verbena, or eat a fruit; there were borders of box, but also of sorrel and chibol; and the stiff battalion of leeks, shallots, and garlic, the delicate pale-green foliage of the carrot, the aggressive steel-grey leaves of the artichokes, the rows of lettuce which always ran to seed too quickly.

———

MARCEL BOULESTIN
MYSELF, MY TWO COUNTRIES

OLD NAMES

Roses…Old names which evoked like poetry
the old gardens of France, of Persia, of Provence…
Belle de Crecy, Belle Isis, Deuil du Roi de Rome,
Rosamunde, Carmaieux, Isphahan.

———

MARY STEWART
THIS ROUGH MAGIC

1

1 – Belle Isis
2 – Isphahan
3 – Rosamunde
4 – Belle de Crecy
5 – Carmaieux

Prince Charles' Postmodern Garden Design for Highgrove

CHATTING THEM UP

I just come and talk to plants really –
very important to talk to them, they respond,
I find.

———

PRINCE CHARLES ON GARDENING
Quoted in the *DAILY MAIL* 1994

The Carpet Garden

ALWAYS A ROSE

The rose is a rose,
And was always a rose.
But the theory now goes
That the apple's a rose,
And the pear is, and so's
The plum, I suppose.
The dear only knows
What will next prove a rose.
You, of course, are a rose –
But were always a rose.

—

ROBERT FROST
THE ROSE FAMILY

GOD'S SIGN

A garden is a lovesome thing, God wot!
Rose plot,
Fringed pool,
Fern'd grot –
The veriest school
Of peace; and yet the fool
Contends that God is not –
Not God! in gardens! when the eve is cool?
Nay, but I have a sign;
Tis very sure God walks in mine.

———

THOMAS EDWARD BROWN

PEAS

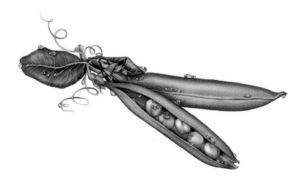

The variety of vegetables grown in the garden were an obligatory source of conversation at dinner at Versailles. As Madame de Sévigné remarks: "The craze for peas continues, the impatience to eat them, to have eaten them, and the pleasure of eating them are the three subjects our princes have been discussing for the last three days."

———

STEPHANIE DE COMTORS
LE POTAGER DU ROI

FLOWERS IN THE RUINS

On the way home I went behind the black ruins where professor K. used to live and broke into his abandoned garden, where I picked several crocuses and tore off some lilac branches.

Took some to Frau Golz, who used to live in my apartment building. We sat across from one another at her copper table and talked. Or rather, we shouted above the gunfire that had just resumed. Frau Golz, her voice breaking: "What lovely flowers, what lovely flowers." Tears were running down her face. I felt terrible as well. Beauty hurts now. We're so full of death.

———

A WOMAN IN BERLIN, 1945

IN ITS SEASON

GOD Almighty first planted a garden. And indeed it is the purest of human pleasures. It is the greatest refreshment to the spirits a man shall never see; without which, buildings and palaces are but gross handiworks; and a man shall never see, that when ages grow to civility and elegancy, men come to build stately sooner than to garden finely, as if gardening were the greater perfection. I do hold it, in the royal ordering of gardens, there ought to be gardens, for all the months in the year, in which severally things of beauty may be then in season. For December, and January, and the latter part of November, you must take such things as are green all winter: holly; ivy; juniper; cypress-trees; yew; pine-apple-trees; fir-trees; rosemary, lavender; periwinkle; the white, the purple, and the blue; germander; flags; orange-trees; lemon-trees; and myrtles, if they be stoved; and sweet majoram, warm set. There followeth, for the latter part of January and February, the mezereon-tree, which then blossoms; crocus vernus, both the yellow and the grey; primroses, anemones; the early tulippa; hyacinthus orientalis; chamairis; fritellaria. For March, there come violets, specially the single blue, which are the earliest; the yellow daffodil; the daisy; the almond-tree in blossom; the peach-tree in blossom; the cornelian-tree in blossom; sweet-briar. In April follow the double white violet; the wallflower; the stock-gilliflower; the cowslip; flower-delices, and lilies of all natures; rosemary-flowers; the tulippa; the double peony; the pale daffodil; the French honeysuckle; the cherry-tree in blossom; the damson and plum-trees in blossom; the white thorn in leaf; the lilac-tree. In May and June come pinks of all sorts, specially the blushpink; roses of all kinds, except the musk, which comes later; honeysuckles; strawberries; bugloss; columbine; the French marigold, flos Africanus; cherry-tree in fruit; ribes; figs in fruit; rasps; vineflowers; lavender in flowers; the sweet satyrian, with the white flower, herba muscaria; lilium convallium; the apple-tree in blossom. In July come gilliflowers of all varieties; musk-roses; the lime-tree in blossom; early pears and plums in fruit; jennetings, codlins. In August come plums of all sorts in fruit; pears; apricocks; berberries; filberds; musk-melons; monks-hoods, of all colors. In September come grapes; apples; poppies of all colors; peaches; melocotones; nectarines; cornelians; wardens; quinces. In October and the beginning of November come services; medlars; bullaces; roses cut or removed to come late; hollyhocks; and such like. These particulars are for the climate of London; but my meaning is perceived, that you may have ver perpetuum, as the place affords.

FRANCIS BACON
ESSAYS

ADDICTION

The love of gardening is a seed once sown that
never dies.

—

GERTRUDE JEKYLL

FLATTERY

"Won't you come into the garden,
I would like my roses to see you."

———

RICHARD BRINSLEY SHERIDAN TO A VISITING
YOUNG LADY

TECHNIQUE

Gardening requires lots of water – most of it in
the form of perspiration.

—

LOU ERICKSON

BONUS

Gardening is cheaper than therapy and
you get tomatoes.

—

ANON.

TOMORROW

He who plants a tree plants a hope.

—

ANON.

IN SPAIN

High above the Alhambra, on the breast of the mountain, amidst embowered gardens and stately terraces, rise the lofty towers and white walls of the Generalife; a fairy palace, full of storied recollections... Here I had an opportunity of witnessing those scenes which painters are fond of depicting about southern palaces and gardens. It was the saint's day of the count's daughter, and she had brought up several of her youthful companions from Granada, to sport away a long summer's day among the breezy halls and bowers of the Moorish palace... Some of the gay company dispersed itself in groups about the green walks, the bright fountains, the flights of Italian steps, the noble terraces and marble balustrades. Others, among whom I was one, took their seats in an open gallery or colonnade, commanding a vast prospect, with the Alhambra, the city and the Vega far below, and the distant horizon of the mountains – a dreamy world, all glimmering to the eye in summer sunshine... The all pervading tinkling of the guitar and click of castanets came stealing up from the valley of the Darro, and half way down the mountain we described a festive party under the trees... some lying on the grass others dancing to the music.

WASHINGTON IRVING
TALES OF THE ALHAMBRA

SEDUCTIVE SHAPES

Gardens should be lovely like well-shaped girls: all curves, secret corners, unexpected diversions and then still more curves.

———

H. E. BATES
A LOVE OF FLOWERS

Alhambra Gardens

Gardening is the most fun you can have with your clothes on.

———

BBC
GARDENER'S QUESTION TIME

UNSATISFACTORY GARDENERS

Josephine's first head gardener was an Englishman, Howatson, whom Napoleon strongly disliked because of his policy, hardly surprising, of planning informal English gardens everywhere. He was quickly replaced by a French expert, Morel, who, alas turned out to be equally unsatisfactory. Moreover he was disposed to go even further afield than Howatson for his models. Morel, it developed, had written not only The Art of Gardening According to Nature, but also The Art of Constructing Gardens According to the Chinese...Following Morel, the distinguished botanist, Mirbel, acted as supervisor of gardens. He too created problems, He became the bête noire of Napoleon, largely because of his ineradicable tendency to spend more than his master had authorised. One year's planning came to double what had been stipulated. The great greenhouse, which was supposed to cost 40,000 francs, actually cost 192,000 francs. Mirbel, moreover, chose to live in considerable state; he had his private quarters at Malmaison and he drove abroad with his own horses and cabriolet. In the Emperor's view this was too much. When dismissal came, Mirbel quickly found a botanist's paradise as intendant for Louis Bonaparte, now King of Holland. One suspects that he obtained this post through Hortense [Josephine's daughter, the Queen of Spain].

—

ERNEST JOHN KNAPTON
THE EMPRESS JOSEPHINE

ONE'S OWN PARADISE

The ancient Persian word *paradaiza* means "the lords' enclosure," referring both to paradise and to a garden, one's own paradise. Similarly, two words the Koran uses for paradise, *firdaws* and *janna*, also mean "garden."

Water is scarce in Persia, so many carpets depict water-gardens, *chahar bagh*, or "quartered gardens." They often show irrigation canals complete with stylized fish.

The crusaders brought back this plan of a square garden divided into four sections, which became popular in Europe.

J.T.

Floral design, Northern India
Mid 17th Century

THE CELESTIAL GARDEN

The eye of love sees behind the roses and the trees, in the shade of the slender cypress and in the modest genuflection of the little violet, in the limpid water of basins and in the gushing fountains faint remembrances of the garden of Paradise with its Tuba tree, kauthar and salsabil; a Paradise which is in turn, only a sensual symbol of God's eye for beauty.

———

ANNEMARIE SCHIMMEL
THE CELESTIAL GARDEN IN ISLAM

Persian miniature, 16th Century

AN OUTING
FOR THE HAREM

When permission was given to the harem to visit the Maybeyn Bahcesi (the gardens of Ceragan Palace in 19th Century Constantinople) the gardeners and watchmen were sent away. Soldiers were posted outside the walls. When the head official of the harem called out "Halvet" (Withdraw), the barred gates to the bridge leading to the road into the park... were opened.

The harem, sometimes accompanied by the sultan himself, sometimes by the princes and princesses, would pass slowly through them. The chief housekeepers of the suites and their private maids would also be present. Then all the ones on duty in other palaces would flood into the garden and scatter on every side. Flitting like butterflies from flower to flower, they would be unconscious of the passing time. In the evening the head official would be heard once more crying "Halvet!" But this time it did not sound so sweet as in the morning. The harsh cry came to separate them from the fresh air of the open woods where they had spent the day in fun and games among the flowerbeds, running and jumping like children in their enjoyment. With drooping heads and dragging feet they came in groups to the bridge and crossed over. After going round the whole area to see that no one had fallen asleep or been left behind, the chief official would close the gates once more.

LEYLA SAZ
HAREM IN ICYUSU

PARITY

A rose by any other name would smell as sweet.

———

WILLIAM SHAKESPEARE

ANECDOTE

I once had a rose named after me and I was very flattered. But I was not pleased to read the description in the catalogue: no good in a bed, but fine up against a wall.

———

ELEANOR ROOSEVELT

RECOGNITION

I once had a sparrow alight on my shoulder for a
moment, while I was hoeing in a village garden,
and I felt that I was more distinguished by that
circumstance than I should have been by any
epaulet I could have worn.

HENRY DAVID THOREAU

THE MOWER

The mower stalled twice; kneeling, I found
A hedgehog jammed up against the blades,
Killed. It had been in the long grass.

I had seen it before, and even fed it, once.
Now I had mauled its unobtrusive world
Unmendably. Burial was no help:

Next morning I got up and it did not.
The first day after a death, the new absence
Is always the same; we should be careful
Of each other, we should be kind
While there is still time.

—

PHILIP LARKIN

HELPING ALONG OLD TAYLOR

This my mother was relating to me in the garden when my father arrived on the scene, in his usual summer rig, with his binoculars slung round him, ready for the distant views. For a moment he surveyed the prospect and for the first time suddenly perceived a construction of, apparently, lattice and flimsy twigs, with some very ostentatious roses trailing about on it. It only escaped being a pergola by its plainly very temporary nature, just as the rambler roses on it only just escaped being Dorothy Perkins.

"Ida, what on earth is that extraordinary thing over there?' he called to my mother, pointing at the object.
"I like colour in the garden, George" she replied, "and I can see it from my bedroom windows, so I told Betts to have the roses planted there as a surprise for you…"
"It certainly has been a surprise! It must be taken down at once. It ruins the whole effect of the garden and, besides, it's just where the wooden tower is to be put up so that I shall be able to see clearly the distant views from the level of the proposed new terrace…"

"To get the full effect of distance I'm afraid I shall have to fell old Taylor's clump over there"'
"But won't he object?" I enquired nervously.
"Really, I can't be expected to ruin all my plans just because an obstinate old man won't cut down a few trees. He'll be lucky, if only he'd realize it, because our woodsman will do it for him–I shall charge him nothing for the labour–and he can sell the timber."

—

OSBERT SITWELL
TALES MY FATHER TAUGHT ME

THE GIANT'S GARDEN

Every afternoon, as they were coming from school,
the children used to go and play in the giant's garden.
It was a large lovely garden, with soft green grass.
Here and there over the grass stood beautiful flowers like
stars, and there were twelve peach trees that in the
springtime broke out into delicate blossoms of pink and
pearl, and in the autumn bore rich fruit. The birds sat on
the trees and sang so sweetly that the children used to stop
their games in order to listen to to them. "How happy we
are here!" they cried to each other.

One day the giant came back. He had been to visit his
friend the Cornish ogre, and had stayed with him for seven
years. After the seven years were over he had said all that
he had to say, for his conversation was limited, and he
determined to return to his own castle. When he arrived
he saw the children playing in the garden.

"My own garden," said the giant; "anyone can understand
that, and I will allow nobody to play in it but myself." So he
built a high wall all round it, and put up a notice-board:

TRESPASSERS
WILL BE
PROSECUTED

He was a very selfish giant.

———

OSCAR WILDE
THE SELFISH GIANT

IRRIGATION

Weather means more when you have a garden.
There's nothing like listening to a shower and thinking how
it is soaking in around your green beans.

MARCELENE COX

CREATING A RED GERANIUM

Imagine that any mind ever thought a red geranium!
As if the redness of a red geranium could be anything but
a sensual experience
And as if sensual experience could take place before there
were any senses.
We know that even God could not imagine the redness of
a red geranium
Nor the smell of mignonette when geraniums were not,
and mignonette neither.
And even when they were, even God would have to have a
nose to smell at the mignonette.
You can't imagine the Holy Ghost sniffing at cherry-pie
heliotrope.
Or the Most High, during the coal age, cudgeling his
mighty brains even if he had any brains: straining his
mighty mind to think, among the moss and mud of lizards
and mastodons to think out, in the abstract, when all was
twilit green and muddy:
"Now there shall be tum-tiddly-um, and tum-tiddly-um,
hey-presto! Scarlet geranium!" We know it couldn't be done.
But imagine, among the mud and the mastodons God
sighing and yearning with tremendous creative yearning,
in that dark green mess oh, for some other beauty, some other
beauty that blossomed at last, red geranium, and mignonette.

—

D. H. LAWRENCE
RED GERANIUM AND GODLY MIGNONETTE

PRIDE OF CREATION

I used to go to revisit it a dozen times a day, and stand in deep contemplation over my vegetable progeny with a love that nobody could share or conceive of who had never taken part in the process of creation. It was one of the most bewitching sights in the world to observe a hill of beans thrusting aside the soil, or a row of early peas peeping out sufficiently to have a line of delicate green.

NATHANIEL HAWTHORNE
MOSSES FROM AN OLD MANSE

THIRSTY SPARROW

There are many beautiful gardens in my part of the world and not one of them has even a sunken bucket in the rockery. They have sweeping lawns, rich conservatories and impeccable borders, but were a thirsty sparrow to land on their estates it would have to put its head through the scullery window to have a drink.

—

BEVERLEY NICHOLS
DOWN THE GARDEN PATH

The sparrow went for a drink.

PAINTING THE ROSES RED

A large rose-tree stood near the entrance of the garden: the roses growing on it were white, but there were three gardeners at is, busily painting them red. Alice thought this a very curious thing, and she went nearer to watch them, and just as she came up to them she heard one of them say, "Look out now, Five! Don't go splashing paint over me like that!"

"I couldn't help it," said Five, in a sulky tone; "Seven jogged my elbow."

On which Seven looked up and said, "That's right, Five! Always lay the blame on others!"

"YOU'D better not talk!" said Five. "I heard the Queen say only yesterday you deserved to be beheaded!"

"What for?" said the one who had spoken first.

"That's none of YOUR business, Two!" said Seven.

"Yes, it IS his business!" said Five, "and I'll tell him – it was for bringing the cook tulip-roots instead of onions."

Seven flung down his brush, and had just begun "Well, of all the unjust things –"when his eye chanced to fall upon Alice, as she stood watching them, and he checked himself suddenly: the others looked round also, and all of them bowed low.

"Would you tell me," said Alice, a little timidly, "why you are painting those roses?"

Five and Seven said nothing, but looked at Two. Two began in a low voice, "Why the fact is, you see, Miss, this here ought to have been a RED rosetree, and we put a white one in by mistake; and if the Queen was to find it out, we should all have our heads cut off, you know.

So you see, Miss, we're doing our best, afore she comes, to – At this moment Five, who had been anxiously looking across the garden, called out "The Queen! The Queen!" and the three gardeners instantly threw themselves flat upon their faces. There was a sound of many footsteps, and Alice looked round, eager to see the Queen.

———

LEWIS CARROLL
ALICE IN WONDERLAND

From Alice in Wonderland

HERESY

"By the way", said Lady Constance, "McAllister speaking to me again last night about the gravel path through the yew alley. He seems very keen on it."

"Glub!" said Lord Emsworth – which, as any philologist will tell you, is the sound which peers of the realm make when stricken to the soul while drinking coffee.

For years Angus McAllister had set before himself as his earthly goal the construction of a gravel path through the Castle's famous yew alley. For years he had been bringing the project to the notice of his employer, though in anyone less whiskered the latter's unconcealed loathing would have caused embarrassment. And now, it seemed, he was at it again.

"Gravel path!" Lord Emsworth stiffened through the whole length of his stringy body. Nature, he had always maintained, intended a yew alley to be carpeted with a mossy growth. And, whatever Nature felt about it, he personally was dashed if he was going to have men with Clydeside accents and faces like dissipated potatoes coming along and mutilating that lovely expanse of green velvet. "Gravel path, indeed! Why not asphalt? Why not a few hoardings with advertisements of liver pills and a filling-station? That's what the man would really like."

Lord Emsworth felt bitter, and when he felt bitter he could be terribly sarcastic.

"Well, I think it is a very good idea," said his sister.

"One could walk there in wet weather then. Damp moss is ruinous to shoes."

P. G. WODEHOUSE
BLANDINGS CASTLE

SWEET HOURS

Where from above the milder sun
Does through a fragrant zodiac run;
And, as it works, th'industrious bee
Computes its time as well as we.
How could such sweet and wholesome hours
Be reckoned but with herbs and flowers!

—

ANDREW MARVELL
THE GARDEN

INTO THE GARDEN

Come into the garden, Maud,
For the black bat, night, has flown,
Come into the garden, Maud,
I am here at the gate alone;
And the woodbine spices are wafted abroad,
And the musk of the rose is blown.

—

ALFRED LORD TENNYSON
COME INTO THE GARDEN, MAUD

MOLE'S GARDEN

The Mole struck a match, and by its light the Rat saw that they were standing in an open space, neatly swept and sanded underfoot, and directly facing them was Mole's little front door, with "Mole End" painted, in Gothic lettering, over the bell-pull at the side.

Mole reached down a lantern from a nail on the wall and lit it, and the Rat, looking around him, saw that they were in a sort of fore-court. A garden-seat stood on one side of the door, and on the other, a roller; for the Mole, who was a tidy animal when at home, could not stand having his ground kicked up by other animals into little runs that ended in earth-heaps. On the walls hung wire baskets with ferns in them, alternating with brackets carrying plaster statuary – Garibaldi, and the infant Samuel, and Queen Victoria, and other heroes of modern Italy. Down one side of the fore-court ran a skittle-alley, with benches along it and little wooden tables marked with rings that hinted at beer-mugs. In the middle was a small round pond containing goldfish and surrounded by a cockle-shell border. Out of the centre of the pond rose a fanciful erection clothed in more cockle-shells and topped by a large silvered glass ball that reflected everything all wrong and had a very pleasing effect.

KENNETH GRAHAME
THE WIND IN THE WILLOWS

AROMA

It was now the sweetest hour of the twenty-four: "Day its fervid fires had wasted" and dew fell cool on panting plain and scorched summit. Where the sun had gone down in simple state – pure of the pomp of clouds – spread a solemn purple, burning with the light of red jewel and furnace flame at one point, on one hill-peak, and extending high and wide, soft and still softer, over half heaven. The east had its own charm of fine, deep blue, and its own modest gem, a solitary star: soon it would boast the moon; but she was yet beneath the horizon.

I walked a while on the pavement; but a subtle, well-known scent – that of a cigar – stole from the window, I saw the library casement open a hand-breadth; I knew I might be watched thence; so I went apart into the orchard. No nook in the grounds more sheltered and more Eden-like; it was full of trees, it bloomed with flowers: a very high wall shut it out from the court on one side; on the other, a beech avenue screened it from the lawn.
At the bottom was a sunk fence; its sole separation from lonely fields: a winding walk, bordered with laurels, and terminating in a giant horse-chesnut, circled at the base by a seat, led down to the fence. Here one could wander unseen. While such

honey-dew fell, such silence reigned, such gloaming gathered, I felt as if I could haunt such shade forever; but in threading the flower and fruit parterres at the upper part of the enclosure, enticed there by a light the now rising moon casts on this more open quarter, my step is stayed – not by sound, not by sight, but once more by a warning fragrance.

Sweetbriar and southernwood, jasmine, pink, and rose, have long been yielding their evening sacrifice of incense: this new scent is neither shrub nor flower; it is – I know it well – it is Mr. Rochester's cigar. I look round and listen. I see trees laden with ripening fruit. I hear a nightingale warbling in a wood half a mile off; no moving form is visible, no coming step audible; but that perfume increases; I must flee. I make for the wicket leading to the shrubbery, and I see Mr. Rochester entering. I step aside into the ivy recess; he will not stay long: he will soon return whence he came, and if I sit still he will never see me.

CHARLOTTE BRONTÉ
JANE EYRE

XANADU

And here were gardens bright with sinuous rills
Where blossomed many an incense-bearing tree...

———

SAMUEL TAYLOR COLERIDGE
KUBLA KHAN

NATURE'S GARDEN

Deer walk upon our mountains, and quail
Whistle about us their spontaneous cries;
Sweet berries ripen in the wilderness;
And, in the isolation of the sky,
At evening, casual flocks of pigeons make
Ambiguous undulations as they sink,
Downward to darkness, on extended wings.

WALLACE STEVENS
SUNDAY MORNING

SWEET SOLITUDE

When I walk alone in the beautiful orchard,
if my thoughts have been dwelling on extraneous
incidents for some part of the time, for some other
part I bring them back to the walk, to the orchard,
to the sweetness of this solitude and to me.

———

MONTAIGNE
ESSAYS

INNISFREE

I will arise and go now, and go to Innisfree,
And a small cabin build there, of clay and wattles
made:
Nine bean-rows will I have there, a hive for the
honey-bee;
And live alone in the bee-loud glade.

———

WILLIAM BUTLER YEATS
THE LAKE ISLE OF INNISFREE

RAPTURE

And after April, when May follows,
And the whitethroat builds, and all the swallows!
Hark, where my blossom'd pear-tree in the hedge
Leans to the field and scatters on the clover
Blossoms and dewdrops – at the bent spray's edge –
That's the wise thrush; he sings each other song
twice over,
Lest you should think he never could recapture
The first fine careless rapture!

ROBERT BROWNING
HOME THOUGHTS FROM ABROAD

THE TURNING POINT

When I awoke, Alice Keach must have been there for some time because she was smiling. "I thought I'd find you here," she said, "when I saw you weren't with the cricketers waiting by the Shepherd. I've brought you a bag of apples. They're Ribston Pippins; they do well up here; I remember you saying you liked a firm apple."

We talked about apples. It seemed that her father had been a great apple man. In Hampshire, they'd had a fair-sized orchard planted with a wide variety and he'd brought her up to discriminate between them. "Before he bit into one, he'd sniff it, roll it around his cupped palms, then smell his hands. Then he'd tap it and finger it like a blind man. Sometimes he made me close my eyes and, when I'd had a bite, ask me to say which apple."

"You mean d'Arcy Spice or Cox's Orange?"

She laughed. "Oh no, that would have been too easy, like salt and pepper. I mean apples very much alike in shape and flavour. Like – well, Cosette Reine and Coseman Reinette. I'm an apple expert. Apples are the only exam I could ever hope to pass."

Then, quite unexpectedly, she asked if she could see my living quarters and we climbed there. "So this is where you spy on us during Sunday services?" she said, poking her head past my baluster and looking down. "What an elevating picture we must make!"

I told her that she'd been safe; I'd only been able to see her hat. "The light straw one," I said. "That's my favourite. Particularly when you stick a rose in the ribbon."

"Stick a rose! Really! Let me tell you, sir, Sara van Fleet isn't any old rose. And it's late in the day to be telling me now. If I'd known, I'd have worn it each Sunday. I don't think Arthur knows what I'm wearing."

Then she turned and went across to the south window. For a while she stood without speaking. Then she said, "So Mr. Moon found it after all?"

Oh, why not? I thought. It's going to be published anyway. So I told her what he'd been doing and leaned forward to point out the site of the Anglo-Saxon chapel. She also turned so that her breasts were pressing against me. And, although we both looked outwards across the meadow, she didn't draw away quite as easily as she could have done. I should have lifted an arm and taken her shoulder, turned her face and kissed her. It was that kind of day. It was why she'd come. Then everything would have been different. My life, hers. We would have had to speak and say aloud what both of us knew and then, maybe, turned from the window and lain down together on my makeshift bed. Afterwards, we would have gone away, maybe on the next train. My heart was racing. I was breathless. She leaned on me, waiting. And I did nothing and said nothing.

She drew back and said shakily, "Well, thank you for showing me. I shall have to hurry away; Arthur will be wondering what's become of me. No, please don't come down."

Then she was gone.

—

J. L. CARR
A MONTH IN THE COUNTRY

COMPULSION

Let no one think that real gardening is a bucolic and meditative occupation. It is an insatiable passion, like everything else to which a man gives his heart.

—

KAREL ČAPEK
THE GARDENER'S YEAR

UNIQUE

No two gardens are the same. No two days are the same in one garden.

—

HUGH JOHNSON

RESISTANCE I

When weeding, the best way to make sure you are removing a weed and not a valuable plant is to pull on it. If it comes out of the ground easily, it is a valuable plant.

———

ANON.

RESISTANCE II

Tomatoes and squash never fail to reach maturity. You can spray them with acid, beat them with sticks and burn them; they love it.

———

S.J. PERELMAN
ACRES AND PAINS, 1951

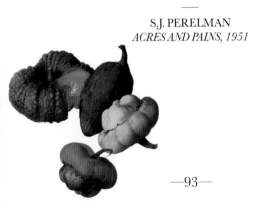

A MIDWIFE'S INVENTORY

Anne also earned money as a midwife and healer, for which she grew a large herb garden. While every woman then grew and distilled herbs for daily use, mostly medicinal, a midwife had more expertise than most. She made syrups, decoctions, lotions, and tonics from the simples (herbs used individually for their curative powers) and worts (those used collectively) in her garden. Among these were betony (to reduce labour pains), columbine (to speed delivery), horehound (to ease labour) tansy (to prevent miscarriage) pennyroyal (to induce abortion), comfrey (to relieve nursing sores), stinging nettle (to increase the flow of breast milk), lady's mantle (an aid to conception and healthy pregnancy), the towering angelica (to ward off the plague), lemon balm (to "purge melancholy," making it, along with lavender, gillyflowers, and thyme, an early antidepressant), clary (its seeds were crushed into a paste to extract thorns), borage (to fortify the heart), heartsease (against syphilis and epilepsy), elecampane (for coughs), garlic (to relieve aches and pains), bugle (to cure nightmares), feverfew (to reduce fever), herb Robert (a diuretic), monkshood (to exterminate rats and other vermin), spearmint ("friendly to a weak stomach") and sage (to quicken the memory). Like Will, Anne spent much of the year outside, planting in spring, weeding in summer, and harvesting in fall.

EVE LA PLANTE
AMERICAN JEZEBEL

DELIGHT

By plucking her petals, you do not
gather the beauty of the flower.
Rabindranath Tagore

What greater delight is there
than to behold the earth
appareled with plants as with a
robe of embroidered works, set
with Orient pearls and garnished
with the great diversitie of rare
and costly jewels. But these
delights are in the outward
senses. The principal delight is in
the mind, singularly enriched with
the knowledge of these visible
things, setting forth to us the
invisible wisdom and admirable
workmanship of almighty God.

JOHN GERARD
THE HERBAL

DAFFODILS

I wandered lonely as a cloud
That floats on high o'er vales and hills,
When all at once I saw a crowd,
A host, of golden daffodils;
Beside the lake, beneath the trees,
Fluttering and dancing in the breeze...

For oft, when on my couch I lie
In vacant or in pensive mood,
They flash upon that inward eye
Which is the bliss of solitude;
And then my heart with pleasure fills,
And dances with the daffodils.

———

WILLIAM WORDSWORTH
DAFFODILS

FULFILLMENT

All gardeners live in beautiful places because they
make them so.

———

JOSEPH JOUBERT

CONSOLATION

How fair is a garden amid the trials and passions
of existence.

———

BENJAMIN DISRAELI

ENRICHMENT

I sometimes think that never blows so red
The rose, as where some buried Caesar bled,
And every hyacinth the garden wears
Dropt in her lap from some once lovely head.

—

EDWARD FITZGERALD
THE RUBAIYAT OF OMAR KHAYAM

THE RETURN OF ODYSSEUS

Old Laertes wept before Odysseus. With his hands he took up the dust of the ground, and he strewed it over his head in his sorrow. The heart of Odysseus was moved with grief. "Behold I am here, even I, my father. I, Odysseus, have come back to mine own country."

Then Odysseus took him through the garden, and he told him of the fruit trees that Laertes had set for him when he, Odysseus, was a little child, following his father about the garden – thirteen pear trees, and ten apple trees, and forty fig trees.

When Odysseus showed him these Laertes knew that it was his son indeed who stood before him – his son come back after twenty years' wandering. He cast his arms around his neck, and Odysseus caught him fainting to his breast, and led him into the house.

———

HOMER
ODYSSEY

HARMONY

The zen garden's sand
And stones; such simplicity –
Subtle and sublime.

—

OWEN JOHNSTON
ZEN GARDEN HAIKU

THE RYOANJI TEMPLE GARDEN

The magic of the Ryoanji Garden is
unlike any other: not only aesthetic but spiritual.
First, like many Japanese gardens, no flowers,
just a sea of gravel, and 14 "islands" of stone.
The gardeners are monks who as a spiritual
exercise rake the gravel from time to time.

To visit the Ryoanji you sit on benches that run
along its edge and gaze out – for hours, it may be
– and let its mysterious harmony work its magic.
Which, over the centuries, for very many, it has.

It is a good candidate for the title of the most
remarkable garden in the world. Even the faded
wall on its far side is considered one of Japan's
great national treasures.

—

J.T.

The Ryoanji Temple Garden
Kyoto, Japan.

THE GLORY OF THE GARDEN

Our England is a garden, and such gardens are not made
By singing "Oh, how beautiful," and sitting in the shade
While better men than we go out and start their working lives
At grubbing weeds from gravel-paths with broken dinner-knives.
There's not a pair of legs so thin, there's not a head so thick,
There's not a hand so weak and white, nor yet a heart so sick
But it can find some needful job that's crying to be done,
For the Glory of the Garden glorifieth every one.

Then seek your job with thankfulness and work till further orders,
If it's only netting strawberries or killing slugs on borders;
And when your back stops aching and your hands begin to harden,
You will find yourself a partner in the Glory of the Garden.
Oh, Adam was a gardener, and God who made him sees
That half a proper gardener's work is done upon his knees,
So when your work is finished, you can wash your hands and pray
For the Glory of the Garden that it may not pass away!

———

RUDYARD KIPLING

Moonbridge at
The Japanese Garden
Huntington, California

JOHN TRAIN

John Train has written hundreds of columns in the *Wall Street Journal*, *Forbes*, London's *Financial Times*, and other publications, as well as over 20 books on many subjects. Also a number of amusing "little books", including *John Train Most Remarkable Names, Most Remarkable Occurences, Wit: The Best Things Ever Said, Love*, and others, which have proven to be perennial popular stocking stuffers.

He has received several appointments from Presidents of both parties. He and his wife live in New York and Maine.

LINDA KELLY

Linda Kelly's previous books include *The Young Romantics, Women of the French Revolution* and most recently *Holland House: A History of London's most Celebrated Salon*. She is a Fellow of the Royal Society of Literature and the Wordsworth Trust. Her husband is the writer Laurence Kelly; they live in London and spend some time in Ireland, where they have a cottage on the Wexford coast.